Cover to Cover Bible Study

7 Sessions for Homegroup and Personal Use

C000193560

2 Corinthians

Restoring harmony

Christine Platt

CWR

Contents

Introduction

The Corinth Paul knew was a bustling, prosperous hub of trade, manufacturing, tourism and religious pilgrimage at the gateway to Europe and Asia. It had been a leading centre of Greek power, but in 44 BC Caesar established it as a Roman colony. Some Greeks still lived there, but in official and public life it was essentially Roman, although the Greek language was still used.

The missionary heart of Paul had leapt at the potential of Corinth. Because of its cosmopolitan populace who travelled widely throughout Greece and the eastern Mediterranean, what was taught there would reach far beyond its borders. He stayed at least eighteen months (Acts 18:1–11) around AD 51–52 and the church flourished. The believers met in homes, probably in groups of 30–50, a figure estimated from excavations of several large houses in Corinth dating from the first century. It is possible that one such cell group met in Stephanas's home (1 Cor. 1:16).

As with any church, the believers were under pressure to conform to the prevailing culture, which was Greco–Roman, and this was fertile ground for difficulties.

Despite having moved on to Ephesus, Paul did not abandon his congregations and was always keen to get news, good or bad, so he could continue his pastoral care among the fledgling churches. It is difficult to reconstruct accurately the timetable of Paul's visits and letters between the writing of 1 and 2 Corinthians, but many scholars agree with the following scenario: Paul had responded to some initial problems and questions from the Corinthian church by letter (1 Cor.). This was written from Ephesus in about AD 53–54. (See *Cover to Cover: 1 Corinthians*). This letter appeared to result in little change among the believers. Paul paid a 'painful visit'

(2 Cor. 2:1) and he later sent a severe letter (2 Cor. 2:3–4,9), delivered by his co-worker Titus, which is now considered to be lost. Paul and Titus then met in Macedonia to discuss the Corinthian believers' response to the severe letter and Paul subsequently wrote another letter – our 2 Corinthians – in AD 55–56.[1]

In the meantime some opponents to Paul – false apostles – had arrived in Corinth and sought to lead the believers astray, so naturally Paul was anxious to get stuck into that.

Reconciliation

One of the major themes of 2 Corinthians is reconciliation. False apostles had denigrated Paul's reputation and enticed the Corinthian believers to doubt his sincerity, his message and even his God-given apostleship. A lesser man might have reacted with anger at such personal attacks, but Paul revealed his humility and largeness of heart as he sought to build bridges between himself and the church at Corinth. It was vital for him to restore their confidence in him as God's apostle.

This humility was in stark contrast to Greco–Roman culture, which emphasised public boasting and self-promotion. Orators were praised for their eloquence and paid to entertain. The truth of what was declaimed was often subservient to the performance itself.

Patronage

Paul was also countercultural in that he refused to accept money for his ministry from the Corinthian believers (2 Cor. 2:17; 12:11–15). He supported himself as a tentmaker and received gifts from other churches (Phil. 4:14–18). Patronage was endemic in Greco–Roman culture. Wealthy influential patrons provided protection and money for poorer clients, expecting these clients to support their patron's political ambitions and publicise their good name. To accept help of this kind would have implied that Paul was in their debt, thus tainting his message.

There were some, not many, well-to-do people in the Corinthian church (1 Cor. 1:26). They may have expected their wealth to give them a position of leadership, especially as the believers met in homes and only the wealthy would have spacious dwellings. Paul was determined to avoid the whole cultural practice of patronage, even though that offended the Corinthians (2 Cor. 11:7–11).

Travel plans
Paul had changed his travel plans (2 Cor. 1:15–18). The 'super apostles' used this to poison the minds of the believers, inferring that Paul was not to be trusted.

A word to the wise
Paul communicated in several ways – in person, by preaching, teaching and in conversations, by sending messengers who knew his heart and could expound on points of difficulty, and also by letters. We are now left with just some of his letters and accounts of a few conversations and sermons. We do not have Paul's total thought on any topic: 2 Corinthians was largely written to deal with specific issues related to that church and is not a complete manual on how to do church. God has provided us with other biblical writings to expand our understanding.

Did that earnestly sought-after reconciliation actually happen? Romans 16:23 gives a significant clue. Paul returned to Corinth and stayed with the believers. From there he wrote the letter to the Romans, sending greetings from leading Corinthian Christians. God's reconciling power working through His servant seems to have healed the breach – an amazing result in such an unhelpful cultural context. We face similar challenges today. But with God's mighty help, we too can demonstrate His love and forgiveness to the sceptical world as we work at being reconciled to one another.

Note

1. Ben Witherington III, *Conflict and Community in Corinth: A Socio-Rhetorical Commentary on 1 and 2 Corinthians* (Grand Rapids: Eerdmans, 1995), pp.352–353.

WEEK 1

I Love You Guys!

Opening Icebreaker

What person of influence – Christian or secular – do you admire the most and why?

Bible Readings

- 2 Corinthians 1:1–2:17
- Hebrews 12:1–15
- Matthew 20:20–28

Opening Our Eyes

Paul's affection for and confidence in these somewhat difficult Corinthian believers pours out from these two chapters. He is grieved by their personal attacks, but his pastoral heart is deeply concerned for their spiritual welfare. He knows he has an uphill battle to win back their friendship, so he starts by taking the spotlight off himself and shines it fully on God (1:2–3). I am constantly amazed at how quick we can be to criticise God's servants. We lose sight of the fact that they belong to God and are precious to Him. God is worthy of our praise, not our criticism of His workers.

From the background of loving concern for them he begins a systematic defence of his apostleship and explanation of his decision-making processes. His first words are: 'Paul, an apostle of Christ Jesus by the will of God ...'. From that standpoint he could have commanded the people to respect and obey him, but he chose the way of patience and love – a salutary example for those in Christian leadership. He had surely learned this lesson from Jesus, who 'did not come to be served, but to serve ...' (Matt. 20:28). Jesus did not bully His disciples into obedience. He earned their devotion by His sacrificial life. There is no place for a domineering bully in God's kingdom.

Paul, like his Master Jesus, was no stranger to suffering. He seemed to have been pushed to the extreme (1:8–10). These traumas had nevertheless become a rich reservoir of learning about why believers suffer.

- The comfort we receive from God enables us to comfort and encourage others (1:5–6).
- Trials will come, but God will deliver us from them or in them (1:8–11).

- Hardship helps to keep us from sin (12:7).
- God uses trials to perfect our character (Rom. 5:1–5).
- We learn to rely on God, not on ourselves (1:9).

Our attitude in suffering needs to be 'patient endurance' (1:6). If we become bitter, critical or resentful our trials will work against us, not for us (Heb. 12:15).

Paul then explains why he changed his plans (1:12–23). Again he identifies himself as God's servant. As God is faithful, Paul also aims to be faithful and sincere in every way. Rather than being fickle, it was out of concern for the Corinthians that he changed his travel plans. It is tough when our best motives are misconstrued.

He is eager to praise the Corinthians for taking his letter to heart and carrying out the discipline of an offender. He is delighted to learn that the man is genuinely sorry and has repented, so now he urges forgiveness and reconciliation.

Paul was acutely disappointed not to find Titus in Troas with news of how the Corinthians had received him (2:12–13). His anxiety was so heavy that he abandoned a promising ministry in order to travel on and find Titus. There is a lesson here for us: open doors may abound, but we need to discern which one God wants us to pursue.

Despite the crushing load of suffering, anxiety and unjust criticism, Paul plumbs the depths of his faith and reaffirms Christ's majestic victory parade (2:14–17) and the believer's privilege of sharing in that victory. The 'aroma' released by our Christian testimony brings life to some by its inviting beauty. To others it carries the smell of death if they refuse to respond to Christ's invitation.

Discussion Starters

1. How does Paul describe God and His work in His people (1:2–3,5,9–12,18,20–22; 2:14,17)? Make a list.

2. In what ways have you experienced any of these aspects of God?

3. What had Paul learned about why believers suffer (see Opening Our Eyes)?

4. Why else do believers suffer (cf. Jonah)?

5. How can you cultivate a more God-honouring attitude to suffering?

_____

_____

_____

_____

6. What qualities of Paul's leadership are demonstrated in these two chapters?

_____

_____

_____

_____

7. Take a few minutes to pray over these qualities for yourself and for leaders in your church community.

_____

_____

_____

_____

Personal Application

Paul was a vulnerable human being just like us. God anointed him for a mighty task and he put his whole heart, soul, mind and strength into it. He kept his relationship with Christ central and did not allow the 'ministry' to crowd out his devotion to Jesus. God has given you the task of being His witness and His servant in your world. No one else can fulfil your specific role. Are you putting all your energy and passion into that?

Despite all the external pressures and busyness, are you keeping your relationship with Christ as first priority? How is your devotional life? Do you need some fresh stimulus? CWR has daily devotional booklets that can help, such as *Every Day with Jesus* and *Inspiring Women Every Day*.[1]

Seeing Jesus in the Scriptures

The twin themes of leadership and suffering bring us face to face with the supreme example of Jesus. He demonstrated servant leadership and yet was not afraid of being upfront and honest when His disciples did not come up to the mark. They accepted His rebuke because they were convinced of His deep love for them. He loves you in the same way. If He has to rebuke you, be assured He is motivated by His compelling desire for you to be the best you can be.

Whatever suffering you might be going through, the spiritual and physical anguish Jesus experienced when clothed with mortal flesh like us is way beyond anything we could ever comprehend. Consequently He is able to understand and empathise with our deepest hurts.

Note
1. For further devotional material, visit CWR's website: www.cwr.org.uk

WEEK 2

Hallelujah – He Has Risen!

Opening Icebreaker

Word association: What are the first five words that come into your mind when you hear the word 'law'? What are the first five words that come into your mind when you hear the word 'Spirit'?

Bible Readings

- 2 Corinthians 3:1–4:18
- Exodus 31:18
- Jeremiah 31:31–34
- Romans 8:1–17

Opening Our Eyes

The law and the Spirit (2 Cor. 3)

Paul distances himself from other itinerant teachers who use letters of recommendation to prove their credentials. He has no need of such letters, which could be obtained fraudulently. The very existence of the church at Corinth is his letter of recommendation. He is still working on restoring his relationship with the Corinthians. He does not boast of his own success, although the culture would encourage that. He makes it clear that it is the Spirit of God who empowers him (3:6).

Talking of letters leads him to contrast the giving of the law at Sinai in letters of stone to the giving of the Spirit written on human hearts. He is not dismissive of the law. It is a glorious gift God gave to His people. The problem was not with the law, but with the people. The law reveals sin. The new covenant, prophesied by Jeremiah and inaugurated by Jesus, enables change from the inside out rather than striving for outward conformity to the law, like the Pharisees in Jesus' time. We should still honour God's law, but rely on Him to work in us through His Spirit to enable us to obey.

Legalism, exemplified by the Pharisees, is defined as 'strict or excessive conformity to the law or to a moral code' (*The New Penguin English Dictionary*). It reveals itself in harsh judgmentalism of others, often over minor matters. A 'holier than thou' attitude is a denial of God's love and grace. Legalism can also be inflicted on ourselves, when we heave onto our fragile shoulders a huge burden of shoulds and ought-tos. The true gospel is characterised by grace and dependence on God to enable us to walk in His ways, forgiving others and ourselves when we fail.

Many observers of Christianity today see only a list of dos and don'ts. What a travesty! Christ-followers are sometimes characterised by what they don't do, rather than what they do. What observers should see is the demonstration of Christ's liberating, transforming power.

The centrality of Christ and His resurrection (2 Cor. 4)

Rather than put himself on a pedestal, Paul places Jesus firmly in the limelight. Although Paul has been 'hard pressed on every side ... perplexed ... persecuted ... struck down' (4:8–9), so that others could hear the truth, he considers these trials to be 'small potatoes' (*The Message*) because he is focused on Christ's resurrection power and the prize of eternal glory in heaven. Despite all, he has not been 'crushed ... in despair ... abandoned ... or destroyed' (vv.8–9). Christ's resurrection power has transformed him as it did the other apostles, who fled in terror in Gethsemane but preached boldly after Pentecost.

Craig Keener expresses it this way: 'Sharing Christ's resurrection life is both a present, internal experience (4:10–11,16) and a future hope (4:14; 5:1–4); both enable Paul to face hardship confidently (4:16; 5:6). Paul's sharing the cross brings his hearers the message of life (4:12).'[1]

Without the resurrection our faith is futile (1 Cor. 15:17). As with all the other religions, we are left with merely a good example of how to live life, but with no power to do it. Jesus has conquered death and broken Satan's power over humanity. Because He has risen, He can guarantee resurrection power to all His followers.

Discussion Starters

1. What are the Ten Commandments God has given?

_____

_____

_____

_____

2. What is Jesus' summary of the Ten Commandments?

_____

_____

_____

_____

3. How does the Holy Spirit help us to obey God's law?

_____

_____

_____

_____

4. In what ways have you experienced the Holy Spirit's help in your endeavours to live as God desires?

_____

_____

_____

_____

Hallelujah – He Has Risen!

5. What are some examples of legalism that you have experienced or fallen into yourself?

_____
_____
_____
_____

6. How could you help someone break free from a legalistic mindset?

_____
_____
_____
_____

7. What enabled Paul to persevere in his God-given task despite many obstacles and personal suffering?

_____
_____
_____
_____

8. How can you draw more on Christ's resurrection power in your own life?

_____
_____
_____
_____

Personal Application

God wants you to embrace Christ's resurrection power. He knows you cannot live fully for Him without it. His desire is that your life will radiate His beauty, truth and grace to a watching world. Pray Psalm 139:23–24 and ask Him to reveal any areas of legalism which are stunting your growth. Then refer to your answers to Question 6 and seek freedom.

Search your heart also about areas where you are holding back out of fear. Do you want Jesus or fear to be your master? Fear is from the enemy. He wants to keep you stuck firmly in your comfort zone. Even tiny steps to break out of entrenched patterns of behaviour that hold you back will be richly rewarded. Live by faith, not by fear (Gal. 2:20).

Seeing Jesus in the Scriptures

When Jesus gave up His earthly life, He declared from the cross, 'It is finished.' The perfect Lamb of God (John 1:29) had 'entered the Most Holy Place once for all by his own blood, having obtained eternal redemption' (Heb. 9:12). The system of sacrifices demanded under the old covenant was finished and we, His followers, 'have been made holy through the sacrifice of the body of Jesus Christ once for all' (Heb.10:10). He has lifted from our shoulders the crushing burden of trying to be good enough. Instead He invites us to share His yoke (Matt. 11:29–30).

The only fitting response to such outrageous love is to worship and offer ourselves as 'living sacrifices, holy and pleasing to God' (Rom. 12:1).

Note

1. Craig S. Keener, *The New Cambridge Bible Commentary, 1–2 Corinthians* (Cambridge University Press, 2005), p.175.

WEEK 3

Reality Check

Opening Icebreaker

Name some storybook characters who had or who took on outward appearances which were very different from their inward qualities.

Bible Readings

- 2 Corinthians 5:1–6:13
- 1 Corinthians 3:10–15
- John 17:20–26

Opening Our Eyes

Resurrection and judgment

Paul's poor earthly body has experienced a lion's share of abuse and he is acutely aware of it groaning. Maybe you identify with him. He longs to get his resurrection body. On earth believers live in vulnerable 'tents'. At death we leave that 'tent' and enter an intermediate state of being without a body – but with the Lord – while we await corporate resurrection into new bodies. 'Paul seems to believe that believers' resurrection bodies are already prepared in heaven, in heavenly cold storage so to speak.'[1]

The life in heaven is the true life (5:5). We are to be 'swallowed up by life' (v.4), not by death. Although we grieve when a believer dies because we are deprived of their friendship, we celebrate as they enter into God's presence. We know we will see them again – with our new resurrection bodies. That conviction, buoyed up by the gift of the Holy Spirit's presence, will keep us from discouragement when life falls apart and disappoints us. This life is temporary – the next one is the real one!

Believers will face judgment – not as a test of whether they are saved, which is established once and for all through faith in Christ (Eph. 2:8–9) – but to examine whether they have served God or wasted their lives, gifts and opportunities (1 Cor. 3:11–15). Paul therefore always aims to please God, trusting that at the judgment seat Christ will vindicate his ministry, whether or not the Corinthians accept him as God's apostle.

Reconciliation

This is 'a renewed state of harmony that exists between previous opposing groups' (*The New Penguin English Dictionary*).

Some of Paul's flamboyant orator opponents appeared to have claimed that their ecstatic experiences were superior to Paul's, thereby 'proving' they were the most spiritual. They were motivated by 'money, popularity and self-importance' rather than by a desire for true spirituality (*NIV Study Bible*, notes for 2 Cor. 5:12). Paul counters them by saying that his deepest spiritual experiences are between himself and God alone. He does not gloat about them to impress others. In 1 Corinthians 14:19 he asserts he would rather speak five intelligible words to instruct others than 10,000 words in tongues. He is motivated by Christ's love for him, not self-aggrandisement. In his aim to be reconciled with the Corinthians, Paul stresses that the content of his message – the gospel – is of prime importance, not the delivery.

To summarise 2 Corinthians 5:18–20: God is the initiator of reconciliation, Christ is the means of it and Paul is the human agent.

Paul sees reconciliation as crucial and urgent. If the Corinthians are not in harmony with him, they are estranged from God and this is deadly dangerous. He fears they may have received 'God's grace in vain' (6:1). For Paul there are no obstacles to this reconciliation. Again he commends his lifestyle for the Corinthians to examine. This is how the life of a servant of God should look:

- Endure with integrity whatever comes (vv.4–6).
- Use God-given equipment for ministry (v.7).
- Do not heed others' reactions (vv.8–9).
- Be rich in Christ, if not in worldly sense (v.10).

Because of all this Paul seeks warmth and open-heartedness from the Corinthians. He calls them children – still immature, needing a father's guidance.

Discussion Starters

1. Knowing that our earthly bodies are temporary, what should be our attitude towards them?

2. How can we ensure that when standing before Christ's judgment seat we will hear the words, 'Well done, good and faithful servant'? (Matt. 25:23)

3. How can we identify people who 'take pride in what is seen rather than in what is in the heart' (5:12) and be on our guard against their influence?

4. What is the believer's responsibility as an ambassador for Christ?

5. What is one thing you can do this week to grow in becoming a more effective ambassador for Christ?

_____

_____

_____

_____

6. In what ways did Paul suffer for the ministry (6:4–5)?

_____

_____

_____

_____

7. What Christlike behaviour did he display (6:4–6)?

_____

_____

_____

_____

8. What God-given equipment did he use (6:7; see also Eph. 6:10–18)?

_____

_____

_____

_____

9. What was the outcome of his ministry (6:8–12)?

_____

_____

_____

_____

Personal Application

Reading of Paul's lifestyle is daunting. His sufferings, persecution and imprisonments, his journeys, his perseverance despite overwhelming obstacles, his intellect and visionary thinking – all had an incalculable impact on the world as he knew it and for 2,000 years since. Surely he was a superman! God certainly said to him, 'Well done.' But what about us?

The key is: 'So we make it our goal to please him ...' (5:9). That is all that is required. Paul had a specific role and so have you – probably very different, but equally significant to God. Make that a daily prayer: 'Lord, I want to please You today in my family relationships, work, social life and church involvement. Empower me by Your Spirit as You did the apostle Paul.'

Seeing Jesus in the Scriptures

Christ's love shines out of these chapters. How many problems would disappear if we truly believed the vastness of His love for us? Any low self-esteem or fear of the future would evaporate into thin air.

Yet what more can He do to show His love? He left the pure beauty of heaven and came to our polluted world – not just for a quick visit, but to live in it with us for 33 years. He submitted to a ghastly death, which held not only the horrors of physical torture, but the spiritual contamination of all of humanity's sin, past, present and future. He did it all, not out of duty or pity, but out of love, and He invites us to 'remain in [His] love' (John 15:9).

Note

1. Ben Witherington III, *Conflict and Community in Corinth: A Socio-Rhetorical Commentary on 1 and 2 Corinthians* (Grand Rapids: Eerdmans, 1995), p.391.

WEEK 4

Contact Without Contamination

Opening Icebreaker

What qualities do you look for in a real friend?

Bible Readings

- 2 Corinthians 6:14–7:16
- Colossians 3:5–14
- 2 Corinthians 12:7–10

Opening Our Eyes

Be separate

The command 'Do not be yoked together with unbelievers' (6:14) has been applied to marriage and choosing business partners or even a dentist! This is not the context here. Paul refers to the mismatch between Christianity and idolatry. Some believers in Corinth still participated in pagan idol feasts. Paul had already addressed this (1 Cor. 10:14–22) and was dismayed that some persisted in this damaging practice. He brings out the stark contrast between believers and unbelievers: light/darkness; God's temple/idols. Participation in pagan worship brings a total clash of loyalty.

God's command to 'be separate' (6:17) refers to a moral separation from sin, not a physical separation from sinners. Sadly, misguided individuals have taken separation to an extreme and imposed isolation on their followers. How should we relate to unbelievers? Warren Wiersbe writes, 'We must practise "contact without contamination".'[1] Jesus is our example. He was 'holy ... set apart from sinners' (Heb. 7:26) and a 'friend of ... "sinners"' (Luke 7:34). On the basis of God's command, 'Be separate', and His promise, 'I will receive you' (6:17), Paul broadens his argument and urges his 'dear friends' (7:1) to:

(a) purify themselves from 'everything that contaminates body and spirit': not only to refrain from idol feasts, but to get rid of anything that spoils their life in Christ;

(b) perfect 'holiness out of reverence for God': make every effort to grow in holy living.

This means not only a negative drawing away, but a positive decision to devote oneself to God. The Pharisees were zealous in expelling from their lives anything that could pollute them, but miserable failures at knowing God and displaying His character. In

Colossians 3:5–14 we are urged not only to put off bad stuff, but to put on good stuff.

Paul's love for and joy in the Corinthians

We are all painfully aware of the heartbreak and difficulty of seeking to restore broken relationships. There are fractured families and dysfunctional churches around us today. Paul is grieved that some Corinthians will not accept him. He continues to affirm his love for them and praises those who responded actively to his 'severe' letter. He confronted the Corinthians with their sin even though he knew it would cause pain. He was delighted and relieved to learn from Titus that the pain had resulted in godly sorrow at least in some. They disciplined the offender and sought to rebuild their relationship with Paul. So he could honestly say, 'I have great confidence in you; I take great pride in you' (7:4). Even though the Corinthians were his problem children, he was quick to praise and affirm wherever possible.

Paul modelled the idea that broken relationships 'can be repaired and strengthened only when people face problems honestly, deal with them biblically and lovingly, and seek to get right with God'.[2] Although Paul again talks about his trials, 'harassed at every turn' (7:5), he was not indulging in a pity party. Rather he stressed that God sent the necessary comfort, in this case Titus, a supportive friend who brought good news. God had also comforted him in previous trials.

- He appeared and spoke encouraging words (Acts 18:9–10).
- He gave grace to endure (12:7–10).

Paul, though highly gifted and motivated, was a normal person who needed comfort and encouragement. God supplied all he needed at the right time.

Discussion Starters

1. What are some pagan influences that we should beware of?

2. Why is Paul so adamant that the Corinthians should not participate in idol feasts in pagan temples?

3. How could you help someone who was taking the command 'be separate' to an extreme?

4. What helps you to have 'contact without contamination' in friendships with unbelievers?

5. What is involved in putting off the bad stuff and putting on the good stuff, eg putting off greed and putting on kindness?

---

6. How can you identify whether someone is displaying godly sorrow or worldly sorrow?

---

7. What key factors are necessary to restore broken relationships?

---

8. How can we be a 'Titus' for others in difficulty?

Personal Application

Healthy plants grow and bear fruit. God's desire is for His people to grow healthily and bear fruit. The Corinthians were not growing as they should and Paul, as God's spokesman, is eager to help them find the way forward to health and abundance in their Christian walk.

Just as a sickly plant is a denial of its true potential, so it is with the follower of Jesus. Can you see areas where you are growing and changing to become more like Him? Or is something holding you back? Examine Colossians 3:5–14 and see what you need to put off and put on to become more the person you were meant to be in God. Take action today, so you can 'bear much fruit'.

Seeing Jesus in the Scriptures

Relationship is embedded in the heart of God's kingdom. The Trinity – Father, Son and Holy Spirit – is bound together in utter unity. When God's relationship with His creation was fractured, He already had a plan prepared to make reconciliation possible. Jesus is all about restoring broken relationships – between us and God and us and each other.

Relationship breakdowns require a mediator – someone who can bring the two parties together and facilitate reconciliation. Jesus is the complete and perfect mediator (1 Tim. 2:5). He makes restoration possible in the most dysfunctional relationship that ever existed – that between Holy God and rebellious humanity. 'God demonstrates his own love for us in this: While we were still sinners, Christ died for us' (Rom. 5:8). Praise be to Him!

Notes

1. Warren W. Wiersbe, *2 Corinthians. Be Encouraged* (Scripture Press Foundation (UK) Ltd, 1987), p.77.
2. Ibid., p.81.

WEEK 5

Freely You Have Received, Freely Give

Opening Icebreaker

Complete this sentence: 'If I had an unexpected windfall, the charity I would most like to support is …'. Explain why.

Bible Readings

- 2 Corinthians 8:1–9:15
- Exodus 16:4–20
- Mark 12:41–44

Opening Our Eyes

The Jewish believers in Jerusalem were literally starving – in dire need of aid to cope with a devastating famine. This has a familiar twenty-first-century ring about it. Mega-disasters flash across our media with sickening regularity. Paul rallies the largely Gentile church in Corinth and other churches in the area to give generously. Apart from meeting physical needs, he hopes this act of kindness will also show the church leaders in Jerusalem the genuineness of his ministry among the Gentiles and thus build greater unity between the two parts of the Early Church – Jewish background and Gentile background believers.

Similarly, as we today give generously to support those in need outside our church community, this reveals to onlookers the genuineness of our faith in a compassionate and magnanimous Jesus. Our claims to love and follow God need to be expressed in concrete action (1 John 3:16–20). Seeing is believing.

What is involved in giving?
- Surrender oneself and one's resources to God (8:5).
- Give even when it hurts (8:1–4).
- Respond to God's superabundant generosity to us (8:9).
- Take a systematic planned approach: sometimes God will surprise us with a spontaneous opportunity to give, but, generally, gifts should be thought through in advance (1 Cor. 16:2; 2 Cor. 9:7).
- Give according to ability, not necessarily percentage (8:12–14; Mark 12:41–44).
- Give with joy (9:7; Luke 19:1–10).
- Give without fanfare (Matt. 6:1–4).

God provided Israel with manna for forty years. Everyone was able to gather sufficient for the day. Any extra that was hoarded (except for the day before the Sabbath) went rancid and stank. If you had too much and did not share it, you could not hide it – everyone could smell it! What do you do with your surplus?

Ben Witherington III makes this deeply challenging observation especially to those of us living in the developed world who often have an embarrassing surplus of money, food, clothing, shelter and entertainment: 'These chapters suggest that what is most revealing about people is what they do with surplus income, whether they spend it mostly on themselves or look for opportunities to be good stewards, helping others.'[1]

Accountability

Those entrusted with money matters, however minor, should be scrupulous in accountability. Paul makes sure that no one can accuse him of mismanagement of these funds. He delegates responsibility for the collection and administration of the gift to proven reliable people like Titus and other brothers designated by the churches, not his own mates. Everything needed to be fully open to inspection.

Churches or groups where financial dealings are the private province of a selected few are in grave danger of accusation, whether or not there is any basis for it. God sees what is going on. He knows whether the people are honest, but other people need to be able to see and examine the accounts (8:16–24). We need to be sure that the organisations to which we give are known to be trustworthy so that the money is used to accomplish the maximum good.

The Corinthians had started to collect money for the Jerusalem church, but for some reason had gone cold on the project. Paul's encouragements had the desired effect: the gift was eventually given (Rom. 15:25–27)!

Discussion Starters

1. What is Jesus teaching from His observation in Mark 12:41–44 (see also 2 Cor. 8:12)?

2. What should our attitude be towards our money and material resources?

3. What criteria should we use when planning our giving?

4. Why is it important to have a systematic plan for giving?

5. What guidelines apply to us today from the experience of the Israelites who received manna in the wilderness?

_____

_____

_____

_____

6. What qualities does Paul highlight in Titus and the other brothers (8:16–24)?

_____

_____

_____

_____

7. What are the results of generous giving?

_____

_____

_____

_____

8. In what ways can you free up more of your resources so you can give?

_____

_____

_____

_____

Personal Application

Money is a wonderful enabling servant, but a tyrannical master. It can rapidly entwine itself around our hearts and stifle generous thoughts and sacrificial impulses. The love of money can turn what should be a joy – giving to help others – into a burden grudgingly carried. Satan knows that if he controls our wallets, he controls our hearts (Matt. 6:21).

Take some time to think through your giving plan: to whom you give, the amount, how often, and your attitude. Repent of any reluctance. Resolve to be a cheerful giver – literally chuckle as you pass the money over! You will be blessed and God will be chuffed (Luke 6:38). Is there an area where you could exercise self-denial so you can give more?

Seeing Jesus in the Scriptures

How did Jesus become 'poor' so that we might become 'rich'? Jesus, as the son of a skilled carpenter and later a working-class craftsman Himself, would not have been living in abject poverty. During His ministry others met His needs (Luke 8:2–3). The poverty He endured was the massive contrast between His life in heaven and His life on earth. We can barely conceive an iota of what He gave up in order to bless humanity – the riches, honour, glory and power He enjoyed. He 'emptied himself' (Phil. 2:6–8) so He could identify with hopeless sinners and take our punishment.

The incalculable benefits we enjoy include peace with God right here and now, certainty of acceptance into heaven and the constant companionship of the Holy Spirit. Hallelujah! What a Saviour!

Note

1. Ben Witherington III, *Conflict and Community in Corinth: A Socio-Rhetorical Commentary on 1 and 2 Corinthians* (Grand Rapids: Eerdmans, 1995), p.427 footnote.

WEEK 6

The Whole Truth and Nothing But the Truth

Opening Icebreaker

What qualities do you look for in a Bible teacher?

Bible Readings

- 2 Corinthians 10:1–11:15
- John 8:32
- 2 Timothy 3:14–17

Opening Our Eyes

In his lengthy letter to this troubled church Paul carefully explains his apostleship and ministry, then urges the Corinthians to share in the offering for the impoverished Christians in Jerusalem. Now he gets to the tough bit – confronting his opponents head on.

Some commentators think the false teachers Paul exposes over-emphasised the role of the Jewish law in the lives of believers. This was like a red rag to a bull for Paul. He had staked his life on the gospel of grace through faith (Eph. 2:8–9), so any whisper of legalism got his hackles up. Other commentators consider that the false teachers stressed the power and glory of Christ and under-emphasised the suffering and apparent weakness of the crucified Lord, '... a Jesus other than the Jesus we preached ...' (11:4).

Whatever they were teaching, it was not the gospel Paul had learned from Jesus and he was determined to defend the truth at all costs. He knew the truth would build up the Corinthians, whereas false teaching would destroy them – the bride for whom Jesus had offered up His precious life.

How careful we need to be about nuances that slither in and undermine the truth. The Corinthians had been seduced by impressive oratory and authoritative presence. In their book there was no room for weakness, vulnerability, suffering or persecution, and yet Jesus experienced all these, and indicated that His followers would not escape them either (John 15:18; 16:1–2).

As already mentioned, the Greco–Roman culture applauded self-praise and self-commendation. In stark contrast, Paul is careful to 'boast in the Lord' (10:17) – not in his social standing, possessions or achievements. He also points out that '... it is not the one who commends himself who is approved, but the one whom the Lord commends' (10:18).

The false teachers claimed that theirs was the true spiritual ministry and that Paul's ministry was defective in some ways (11:4–6). Warren Wiersbe gives some helpful points in how to measure true spiritual ministry:

(a) 'Am I where God wants me to be?' (10:13–14): Paul's 'field' was ministry to the Gentiles and to go where no one else had been before. He was a true pioneer.
(b) 'Is God glorified by my ministry?' (10:15–17): Is His kingdom being extended?
(c) 'Can the Lord commend my work?' (10:18).[1]

Clearly the intruders into the Corinthian church did not meet these criteria. They had invaded Paul's patch. They had created division in the church, slandered Paul's name and undermined his authority. These '... false apostles, deceitful workmen ...' (11:13) had no chance of being commended by God.

Paul pleads with those who had joined the rebel group – the Corinthian believers who sided with the false apostles – to recognise that he was the one who truly loved them and wanted the best for them (11:2–3,11).

The Corinthian believers were not being obtuse or stupid. But they had allowed themselves to lose sight of the truth. They had been too impressed by externals (10:7). We can easily fall into the same pit.

May God give us the discernment to assess rightly the teaching we receive. Also may God help us to place our own convictions humbly under the scrutiny of godly people so that we are never guilty of spreading malignant teaching to poison the minds and lives of God's precious bride (11:2).

Discussion Starters

1. In what ways did Jesus display meekness and gentleness (10:1)?

_____
_____
_____
_____

2. Why does Paul in this instance stress the meekness and gentleness of Christ rather than His power, authority and majesty?

_____
_____
_____
_____

3. What weapons is Paul referring to in 10:4?

_____
_____
_____
_____

4. In what ways is the mind a battlefield (11:3)?

_____
_____
_____
_____

5. What strategies did Satan use in his interactions with Eve (Gen. 3:1–7)?

_____

_____

_____

_____

6. How can we protect our minds from negative influences?

_____

_____

_____

_____

7. If we discern that some teaching we receive is unbiblical, how should we respond?

_____

_____

_____

_____

8. If we are challenged about the accuracy of any of our convictions, how should we respond?

_____

_____

_____

_____

Personal Application

'What is truth?' asked Pilate. Today people continue to pose the same question. Many decide that 'truth' is whatever fits in with their own wants and needs. 'For the time will come when men will not put up with sound doctrine. Instead, to suit their own desires, they will gather around them a great number of teachers to say what their itching ears want to hear' (2 Tim. 4:3).

Yet Jesus claimed that He is 'the way and the truth and the life' (John 14:6). Relationship with Him on the basis of Scripture should be the foundation of our lives. Are you taking every opportunity to build on your knowledge, understanding and obedience of God's Word, or do you have 'itching ears' and want to hear what suits you?

Seeing Jesus in the Scriptures

Paul refers to Christ being the husband of His bride, the Church. This is an intimate picture of Jesus' relationship with His people (Rev. 19:7). It conveys joy, being cherished, especially chosen for His delight. It implies protection, provision and complete commitment to His bride's total well-being. There is a promise of permanence. This is a relationship which will last throughout all eternity. What an extraordinarily wonderful 'husband'!

In return He asks that His bride be as a 'pure virgin', single-minded in devotion to Him, not allowing anyone else to win her allegiance. As in any marriage, it is the only way this 'marriage' can work. '... as a bridegroom rejoices over his bride, so will your God rejoice over you' (Isa. 62:5b).

Note

1. Warren W. Wiersbe, *2 Corinthians. Be Encouraged* (Scripture Press Foundation (UK) Ltd, 1987), pp.115–118.

WEEK 7

It's a Gift, Not a Handicap

Opening Icebreaker

In the New Testament, who received a vision or angelic visit from God?
Also in the New Testament, what type of suffering did the early Christians endure?

Bible Readings

- 2 Corinthians 11:16–13:14
- John 15:18–25; 16:1–4

Opening Our Eyes

Occupational hardships of ministry

Paul's list of sufferings in 11:23–29 indicates that in Acts
we have only a limited account of his missionary career.
He had a rough time! He 'boasts' about his sufferings and
humiliations, not his successes – a sharp contrast to those
who paraded their accomplishments to impress others.

Paul implies that this is the 'normal' Christian experience.
In parts of our world believers are mercilessly persecuted
and suffer martyrdom. What occupational hardships are
you encountering? Tiredness? Ridicule? Not feeling part of
the 'in-crowd'? Are you choosing to deny yourself some
treats and live simply so you can reflect Jesus' lifestyle
more closely and free up more of your resources for
others? Probably not many of us risk being stoned or
beaten, but let's not settle for a cosy lifestyle which does
not stretch us or compel us to lean heavily on God's grace.

Visions and thorns

If the Corinthians had not been so impressed with ecstatic
experiences, Paul might never have mentioned his own.
Even so, he writes as though it happened to someone
else, so reluctant is he to draw attention to himself.
He is, however, quick to mention his 'thorn'. No one
really knows what this was, but it seems to have been a
persistent physical difficulty, maybe an eye problem.

The key verse to refute 'health/wealth' teaching is 12:9,
and it is an example of how to cope with sufferings.
The Message version reads, 'I quit focusing on the
handicap and began appreciating the gift. It was a case
of Christ's strength moving in on my weakness.' God's
grace was sufficient – not grace for healing, but grace
to endure. Madame Guyon, a French mystic, wrote to a
suffering friend, 'Ah, if you knew what power there is
in an accepted sorrow!'[1] An unaccepted sorrow leads to

bitterness and resentment (Heb. 12:15). A hardened heart cripples relationships with God and others, whereas an accepted sorrow opens the way for God's power to flood in.

Give yourselves regular check-ups
(13:5, *The Message*)

As Paul closes this letter, he warns the Corinthians to get their act together – to test out whether they are walking with God or not – and deal with their problems. If they had followed Jesus' instructions in Matthew 18:15–20 about relationships between believers, these issues (12:20–21) would have been cleared up when they were small instead of ballooning into major clashes.

His final challenge reiterates the main theme of reconciliation between them and God and Paul and each other: 'Aim for perfection, listen to my appeal, be of one mind, live in peace.' This is followed by a stunning promise: '... the God of love and peace will be with you' (13:11). Is it obvious to others by the way we live that the God of love and peace is with us?

We need every Person of the Trinity to enable us to live for God and to be His witness to a watching world, so Paul ends his letter with this stupendous statement: 'The amazing grace of the Master, Jesus Christ, the extravagant love of God, the intimate friendship of the Holy Spirit, be with all of you' (13:14, *The Message*).

May God enable us to grasp more of how amazing the grace of Jesus is, how extravagant God's love is, and to deepen our intimate friendship with the Holy Spirit.

Discussion Starters

1. What 'occupational hazards' do believers in your neighbourhood experience (see Opening Our Eyes)?

_____

_____

_____

_____

2. How would you help someone who was discouraged and upset about the occupational hazards they were experiencing – eg a student being ridiculed for their faith?

_____

_____

_____

_____

3. How does 'health/wealth' teaching manifest itself in the Church today?

_____

_____

_____

_____

4. How do you think Jesus would respond to someone who was proclaiming 'health/wealth' teaching?

_____

_____

_____

_____

5. What effect did the 'thorn' have on Paul?

_____

_____

_____

_____

6. What helped him transfer this weakness into strength?

_____

_____

_____

_____

7. How can we give ourselves spiritual check-ups?

_____

_____

_____

_____

8. What would characterise a person who had the God of love and peace dwelling in them?

_____

_____

_____

_____

Personal Application

Paul lived life on the edge. He experienced triumph and tragedy, victory and vulnerability. The more he lived on the edge, the closer and richer was his friendship with Christ. When nearing the end of his earthly life, he had no regrets about missed opportunities. He was confident he had 'finished the race' (2 Tim. 4:7).

How about you? Are you pushing the boundaries of knowing God and living for Him each day? Can you step up a notch in your walk with God? Maybe an attitude needs to change: meditate on 'the power there is in an accepted sorrow'. Consider making a simpler lifestyle choice. You only have one chance of life here on earth. Aim to live it in full surrender to the One who loves you so.

Seeing Jesus in the Scriptures

'The amazing grace of the Master, Jesus Christ … be with all of you' (13:14, *The Message*). 'You are familiar with the generosity of our Master, Jesus Christ. Rich as he was, he gave it all away for us – in one stroke he became poor and we became rich' (8:9, *The Message*).

All we possess, both spiritually and materially, we have received from Him as beautifully wrapped presents, purchased at unimaginable cost. Each day He showers us with new gifts to unwrap and discover.

Although 'thank you' seems a pathetic response to such lavish and undeserved bounty, let's make sure that our lives radiate the constant refrain of 'thank You' to our Master Jesus.

Note

1. Warren W. Wiersbe, *2 Corinthians. Be Encouraged* (Scripture Press Foundation (UK) Ltd, 1987), p.142.

Leader's Notes

Week 1: I Love You Guys!

Aims of the Session
1. To set the scene for a clearer understanding of the whole letter.
2. To clarify the importance of loving relationships within the Church.
3. To deepen understanding of why suffering happens and how to cope.

Opening Icebreaker
The aim of this icebreaker is to get people thinking about what makes a good leader. It is also intended to help people feel comfortable with speaking out.

Reading the Introduction to this study guide gives important background to understanding this letter. If your group members have not read it, give them a few minutes to do that before starting the discussion. Also give them time to read the Opening Our Eyes section if they have not already done so.

Bible Readings
Hopefully the group will have read 2 Corinthians 1:1–2:17 before they come to the study. They will have opportunity to skim through it as they answer Question 1.

It would be good to get a couple of people to read the other two references, Hebrews 12:1–15 and Matthew 20:20–28.

Discussion Starters
1. There are at least twenty points to be found about God in these two chapters. Give people plenty of time to find them. It would be helpful to have someone write them up on a black- or whiteboard or to record them in some way

so that the group can see them. They will then be able to respond more easily to Question 2.

2. Linked to Question 1, as outlined above.

3. These are outlined in Opening Our Eyes. It would be good to encourage people to share what they have learned from the sufferings they have experienced.

4. Jonah's own sin and rebellion brought suffering to him as well as danger to the other sailors. Our sin always has negative consequences for us and those around us.

5. Review the answers to Question 3. Ways of cultivating a more God-honouring attitude to suffering include:
- deciding to trust God and not complain
- focusing on growth through suffering (Rom. 5:1–5)
- recognising that trials are part of life
- asking others to pray with and for you.

6. Paul's leadership qualities include:
- humility – he pointed people to God, not himself
- the ability to encourage and praise the believers
- recognition of his own need of team support (2:12–13)
- honesty and sincerity (2:17)
- patience and clear explanations.

7. Some people may feel that they are not leaders, so this does not apply to them. However, it would be good to point out that we are all in a position of influencing others even if we do not have an official leadership role. You may find that looking at these leadership qualities may show up deficiencies in the leaders in your church community. It is very important to stop at this point and pray for your leaders.

Personal Application
Take time for the group members to think about the

Personal Application section and to share their response. It would be good to have some copies of devotional booklets available for people to borrow.

As you close, encourage the group to read through the whole letter, possibly in a translation they are not so familiar with, and especially focus on the next two chapters, 3 and 4.

Week 2: Hallelujah – He Has Risen!

Aims of the Session
1. To gain a clearer understanding of the implications of the new covenant.
2. To learn how to take hold of Christ's resurrection power in our own lives.

Opening Icebreaker
It is helpful to have paper and pencils so that people can write down their words. Once people have finished 'law', share around the group and then continue with 'Spirit'. This icebreaker is a lighthearted way to get people's minds focused on these two topics.

Bible Readings
Hopefully the group will have read 2 Corinthians 3:1–4:18 before they come to the study.

Ask a couple of people to read the other references, Exodus 31:18; Jeremiah 31:31–34; Romans 8:1–17.

Discussion Starters
1. See how many of the Commandments people can remember before giving them the reference – Exodus 20:1–17.

2. Again, see if the group members remember this –
Matthew 22:37–40.

3. The Holy Spirit helps in various ways:
- Through our conscience when we are tempted to sin,
  and also by conviction of sin when we have fallen.
- He gives power to deny selfish desires and
  resist temptation.
- He provides a way out (1 Cor. 10:13).
- He gives wisdom to make right choices.

4. The group members will learn much from each other
as they share their victories and possible failures.

5. Legalistic thinking often involves rules about Christian
conduct – what Christians should or should not wear (this
often seems to be directed specifically at women); what they
should or should not do – ie dancing, smoking, drinking
alcohol. It can also affect a believer's devotional life – eg 'If
I do not have a Quiet Time, my day will be ruined because
God is not pleased.' Extreme legalism can result in complete
separation from the world, more often seen in cults. It is
important not to let the group become too negative about
this – just stating the situation is sufficient.

6. To break free from a legalistic mindset, a person needs
revelation that they have a legalism problem. Then they
need to repent of it and realise that God's desire is that
they obey Him out of love, not duty or fear (1 John 4:18).
It helps to meditate on and learn an appropriate scripture,
eg 2 Corinthians 3:17, or Romans 8:1–2. Also pray for a
deeper understanding of God's grace (Eph. 2:8–9).

7. Paul was enabled to persevere in his God-given task
because:
- he was convinced that God had called him to this work
  (4:1);
- he knew himself as God's servant (4:5);

- he was convinced of the truth of the gospel (4:6), which is so important that it is worth every sacrifice;
- despite his personal weaknesses, he knew he could rely on Christ's extraordinary power (4:7);
- he recognised that following Jesus will inevitably involve suffering (4:10–12);
- he was aware of the eternal reward – eternity with Jesus (4:14,17);
- his love for others, especially the Corinthian believers, enabled him to keep going (4:15);
- he focused his mind on unseen realities rather than day-to-day problems (4:18).

8. To draw on Christ's resurrection power in our own lives, apart from following Paul's good example, we need to pray for God's help. Meditating on and learning scripture can help, eg 2 Corinthians 4:7. We also need to be willing to step outside our comfort zone.

Week 3: Reality Check

Aims of the Session
1. To understand that Christians will be judged on the way they have lived their lives.
2. To understand the need to be discerning when evaluating people.
3. To make a practical application to grow in becoming an ambassador for Christ.

Opening Icebreaker
The aim of this icebreaker is to show that outward appearances can be very deceptive. Some possible answers could be: the witch in the *Narnia* chronicles, the enchantress and the beast in *Beauty and the Beast*, the wolf in *Little Red Riding Hood*, Shrek etc.

Bible Readings

Hopefully the group will have read 2 Corinthians 5:1–6:13 before they come to the study. Ask a couple of people to read the other references, 1 Corinthians 3:10–15 and John 17:20–26.

Discussion Starters

1. We need to keep a good balance here. We are urged to 'lay down our lives' for others (John 15:13), and to give ourselves unsparingly in God's service (Isa. 58:10). We are also urged to honour our body as the temple of the Holy Spirit (1 Cor. 6:19–20), which implies looking after it. This has implications for a healthy lifestyle – protecting our body so that we live as healthily as possible for as long as possible. The balance is also in not being so over-protective of our health and well-being that we draw back from taking risks that God invites us to take.

2. It is very important to stress that Christ's judgment of believers is not a question of salvation – that is assured – but of how we have lived our lives. Some points to bring out:
- daily walking in obedience – being quick to confess and turn away from sin;
- asking for the Holy Spirit's guidance in how to fully use our gifts;
- playing our part in building God's kingdom – this will involve assessing priorities, as well as attitude;
- seeing all of life – family, work, social – as coming under God's authority, not just Christian activities.

3. We need to recognise that there are people coming into churches who aim to deceive, so we should not be too gullible. We need to observe the fruit of their lives. In the case of the Corinthians, these false teachers brought disunity. It is important to be very careful about requests for money, and give to reputable organisations where there is clear accountability.

4. An ambassador for Christ needs to:
- represent Him as truly as possible, so needs a close relationship with Him;
- encourage reconciliation between God and those not yet His people: be ready to share your own story and provide resources that might help – books, DVDs, videos, tracts, etc – and be a friend.

5. Help group members to be realistic and practical in what they plan to do during this week in response to this question. Write down everyone's responses, so you can ask them about it the following week. Some suggestions: they could write out their testimony and pray for an opportunity to share it; they could pray for unbelieving friends and family and look for ways to serve them. As a group you could arrange a social event and invite friends. You could consider what books, DVDs and tracts you could make available to lend to others.

6 – 8. Ask someone to read out these verses and draw out the answers.

9. The outcome of Paul's ministry was mixed! There was glory and dishonour, etc. We need to expect obstacles and hindrances, as well as successes.

Week 4: Contact Without Contamination

Aims of the Session
1. To understand the danger inherent in pagan spiritual practices.
2. To understand how to have 'contact without contamination'.
3. To make a practical decision to put off bad stuff and put on good stuff.

Opening Icebreaker

This icebreaker relates to Titus being a good friend to
Paul and Paul being a good friend to the Corinthians.
Some important qualities are honesty, willingness to
confront, acceptance, encouragement, just being there –
also to have fun!

Bible Readings

Hopefully the group will have read 2 Corinthians 6:14–7:16
before they come to the study. Ask a couple of people
to read the other references, Colossians 3:5–14 and
2 Corinthians 12:7–10.

Discussion Starters

1. This includes any type of occultism: Satanism,
horoscopes, mediums, fortune-tellers, white witches, spirit
guides, crystals that purport to offer healing. Some of
these are bogus, but you can run the risk of opening the
door to Satan and his minions.

2. Some may have thought it was harmless fun and a way
of maintaining friendships. We can be tempted to think
similarly, eg about horoscopes or mediums on television,
and to think it is just a bit of fun. Paul considers anything
to do with paganism a clash of loyalty and a way in for
exploitation by Satan.

3. Some suggestions:
• Point to Jesus' example (Heb. 7:26; Luke 7:34).
• Show them Jesus' prayer in John 17:13–18 where He
  asks His Father not to take believers out of the world,
  but to protect them from the evil one.
• Show them Jesus' command in Mark 16:15: 'Go into all
  the world and preach the good news to all creation.'
NB In regard to marriage, in 1 Corinthians 7 Paul teaches
that if a believer is already married to an unbeliever, they
should stay together, ie not separate.

4. Some starting points:
- Develop prayer and devotional life and be alert to the Holy Spirit's prompting if thinking or values are being compromised.
- Have a good balance between Christian friends and activities and unchurched friends and activities.
- If possible, take a believing friend with you into your secular environment.

5. The key is the mind. We need to remind ourselves who we are: '... God's chosen people, holy and dearly loved ...' (Col. 3:12). Our behaviour needs to be rooted in our identity. We also need to ask God to search our hearts and minds (Psa. 139:23–24) and to reveal anything of which we need to repent.
Example – put off greed:
- repent of it;
- ask others to pray for us;
- start to exercise self-control – deny self one thing each day.

Example – put on kindness:
- on the basis of your identity, aim to do one kind thing each day.

6. Godly sorrow will bring repentance, an acknowledgment of having done wrong, and lead to a changed life. Worldly sorrow is revealed by being sorry for being found out, making excuses for behaviour, not accepting responsibility, and no permanent change.

7. You might like to consider the following:
- prayer;
- both parties need to seek to get right with God;
- honesty – be willing to confront, '... speaking the truth in love ...' (Eph. 4:15);
- willingness on both sides to engage in the process of reconciliation;

- willingness on both sides to accept responsibility for their part in the problem;
- willingness on both sides to forgive;
- both parties need good supportive friends.

8. Emphasise the following points:
- be there – visit, phone, write;
- bring good news – that God loves them and there is a way through;
- point them to God's promises, eg 12:9.

Week 5: Freely You Have Received, Freely Give

Aims of the Session
1. To understand the biblical criteria in relation to giving.
2. To understand the blessings and benefits that come from giving.
3. To make a plan in relation to giving.

Opening Icebreaker
The aim of this icebreaker is to see what is on people's hearts and to prepare the way for greater giving in response to Question 8.

Bible Readings
Hopefully the group will have read 2 Corinthians 8:1–9:15 before they come to the study. Ask a couple of people to read the other references, Exodus 16:4–20 and Mark 12:41–44.

NB Discussions about money can put people on the defensive. It might be good to highlight Paul's comment in 8:12, that 'the gift is acceptable according to what one has, not according to what he does not have'.

Discussion Starters

1. Giving needs to be unostentatious. The rich 'threw in large amounts', which gives the impression that they were playing to the audience, whereas the widow 'put in' her offering (Mark 12:41–42.) The value of the gift to God is not the amount, but the sacrifice and self-denial that the gift represents. The tiniest offering is still precious to Him, even though the amount may seem insignificant.

2. Consider the following:
- We are stewards – all we have has been given by God, and is not our own (Deut. 8:17–18).
- Know your financial position. Keep accurate records on income and expenditure.
- Share with anyone in need, not just believers (Matt. 5:44–48).
- Money is to be our servant, not our master (1 Tim. 6:10).
- Cultivate an attitude of contentment (1 Tim. 6:6–10). This is highly countercultural and needs constant vigilance. Do not get sucked into watching ads on television. You might start to think you actually need what they are trying to sell to you!

3. Some suggestions:
- Surrender self and all resources to God first.
- All giving needs to be a response to God's gift of Jesus to us – therefore, we give with joy and gratitude.
- Draw up a budget – get help with this if you need to.
- Be generous (9:6).
- Consider local needs – church and community – and also overseas needs.
- Be discerning – give to reputable organisations.

4. Haphazard giving may mean you cannot meet your own commitments or that you give only meagre amounts. Your church and other organisations you support also need to be able to budget for the future, so they need to know what amounts they can count on receiving from you.

5. Guidelines might include:
- Acknowledge that all we have comes from God.
- God's plan is for equality.
- Work is important. The Israelites had to gather and cook the manna – it did not arrive as neatly packaged loaves. It required work for those who were able, who could then share with those unable to work.
- Hoarding surplus stuff will have a negative effect (Prov. 11:24).

6. Heart concern for others, enthusiasm and zeal. They took initiative, had a good reputation for service, were supportive fellow workers and their lives honoured Christ. You could take a few moments to pray over these qualities for yourselves and your leaders.

7. Consider:
- Others see the reality of our faith.
- Others are helped – God's kingdom is extended.
- People give thanks to God.
- God will bless, maybe not materially, but in some way.

8. Do your best to earn what you can, without putting yourself or your family under undue pressure, and spend less – adopt a simpler lifestyle.

Week 6: The Whole Truth and Nothing But the Truth

Aims of the Session
1. To be equipped to recognise Bible teachers and to become Bible teachers who correctly handle the word of truth (2 Tim. 2:15).
2. To recognise and to be able to refute wrong emphases and teaching.

Opening Icebreaker

Some qualities to bring out would be: sincerity, humility, knowledge of the Bible and authenticity in living out their message, as well as ability to communicate with the audience.

Bible Readings

Hopefully the group will have read 2 Corinthians 10:1–11:15 before they come to the study.

Ask a couple of people to read the other references, John 8:32 and 2 Timothy 3:14–17.

Discussion Starters

1. Jesus displayed meekness and gentleness in His dealings with children, with the woman caught in adultery, with Peter after his denial, and during His arrest, trial and crucifixion. He came as a servant (Mark 10:35–45). He claimed to be gentle and humble (Matt. 11:29).

2. Paul stresses this because:
- he wanted to give the Corinthians a fully rounded picture of Christ;
- he wanted to show these same qualities when he visited the Corinthians – he did not want to be the stern apostle, bringing discipline, although he was willing to do that if it proved necessary.

This is the best approach to resolving conflicts – to act with meekness and gentleness rather than going in with guns blazing. 'A gentle answer turns away wrath, but a harsh word stirs up anger' (Prov. 15:1).

3. See Ephesians 6:10–18. Weapons are prayer, the Word of God, love and the Spirit of God, not human reasoning or arguments.

4. Our minds exercise a powerful influence on our behaviour. What we think will determine our actions. Satan

is the father of lies (John 8:44), and he will use anything or anybody to infiltrate doubt into believers' minds.

5. Strategies included the following:
• He appeared as a benign being. Eve was not frightened or repulsed by him appearing as a snake.
• He started by sowing doubt in her mind, not with a frontal attack: 'Did God say...?'
• He appealed to her human appetite: 'fruit good to eat', 'you will be like God'.
• He then contradicted God's word.
You could ask the group in what ways they have experienced Satan influencing their minds – possibly the rationalising of sin.

6. Some suggestions:
• We need to immerse our minds in Scripture (Psa. 119:9–11; 2 Tim. 3:14–17; Psa. 1:1–6).
• We need to be discerning in how to interpret it (2 Tim. 2:15).
• We need to be diligent in controlling what input we allow into our minds – films, books, music, gossip. This does not mean that anything that is not Christian is bad and to be avoided. It means that we should not be gullible and blindly allow our minds to be influenced negatively, but we should be discerning and recognise the effect that certain media have on our minds.

7. We need to check our understanding of Scripture. Pray, seek wisdom, ask other spiritual leaders without criticising the original person. If appropriate and possible, talk with the individual about it – '... speaking the truth in love ...' (Eph. 4:15). If there is no resolution, be extra alert and, if possible, avoid being under that person's teaching and influence.

8. The group may have other points to add here:
• We need to receive the criticism with a humble, teachable attitude.

- We need to check our convictions with Scripture and other wise teachers.
- We need to go back and discuss with the individual and, if we are wrong, admit it. If we are right, we should gently give the basis and evidence for our convictions. Stick with what we believe, whether they accept it or not.

Week 7: It's a Gift, Not a Handicap

Aims of the Session
1. To grow in understanding of how to cope in a godly way with suffering.
2. To understand how to give oneself regular spiritual check-ups.

Opening Icebreaker
The aim of this icebreaker is to recognise that Paul, although enormously influential, was not a one-off anomaly in Christian experience. Several received visions and angelic visits and most experienced suffering.

Visions and angelic visits: Zechariah, Mary, Luke, Jesus' Transfiguration, women at the tomb, Stephen, Ananias, Peter, John, Paul.

Sufferings: Stephen, the whole Church (persecuted and dispersed, probably lost possessions, became refugees), Peter, John (imprisoned, exiled). Many travelled around visiting churches – with the inherent dangers and lack of comfort.

Bible Readings
Hopefully the group will have read 2 Corinthians 11:16–13:14 before they come to the study. Ask someone to read the other references, John 15:18–25 and 16:1–4.

Discussion Starters

1. Consider what believers in different age groups might experience in your culture and context, eg school pupils, business owners, families, older people.

NB Whereas we should not go looking for occupational hazards, if we are not experiencing anything like that, then we need to reflect on our lifestyle to see whether we need to make changes and be less 'comfortable'.

2. You could take other examples if this would be more appropriate to your group.
- Empathise with them how hard that is.
- Encourage them to include other believers in their circle of friendships.
- Pray with and for them.
- Explain that this is part of following Jesus (John 15:18) and that Jesus Himself will help them as they keep close to Him.

3. There is an element of truth in this teaching, but the danger is in over-emphasis and not being balanced with all of Scripture. Some examples of such imbalance are:
- 'name it and claim it';
- people being accused of lack of faith if they are not healed after prayer;
- church growth schemes or discipleship programmes which virtually guarantee results if properly followed;
- materialism.

4. Jesus would respond with love. He would point them to His own earthly life and that of many of His followers. He would also challenge them to know His word more deeply and not lead others astray.

5. Some suggestions:
- It limited him, and may have been painful.
- It was something he yearned to get rid of.
- It drove him to prayer for its removal.

6. Prayer helped him. He recognised that although it was a messenger from Satan, God had allowed it. After three responses from God, he accepted it and refused to become bitter. He embraced God's grace, and eventually he delighted in it, not just showing stoic endurance.

7. The fundamental question is: 'Is Jesus in my heart – have I asked for forgiveness and invited Him in as Saviour and Lord?' People can attend church for years and still not bow the knee. For Christians, a spiritual check-up includes asking questions like:
• Am I growing in knowledge and understanding of God's Word?
• Is my prayer life developing?
• Am I learning more about how to be His witness?
• Am I using my gifts in service?
• Am I asking God to reveal sin, so I can repent (Psa. 139:23–24)?
This can be a helpful exercise every three to six months. It could be discussed with a trusted friend.

8. There would be love for God, and for others, especially the unlovely, a joyful attitude to life, not complaining or criticising, a peaceful spirit, not being anxious or worried.

NATIONAL DISTRIBUTORS

UK: (and countries not listed below)
CWR, Waverley Abbey House, Waverley Lane, Farnham, Surrey GU9 8EP.
Tel: (01252) 784700 Outside UK (44) 1252 784700 Email: mail@cwr.org.uk

AUSTRALIA: KI Entertainment, Unit 21 317-321 Woodpark Road, Smithfield, New South Wales 2164.
Tel: 1 800 850 777 Fax: 02 9604 3699 Email: sales@kientertainment.com.au

CANADA: David C Cook Distribution Canada, PO Box 98, 55 Woodslee Avenue, Paris, Ontario N3L 3E5.
Tel: 1800 263 2664 Email: swansons@cook.ca

GHANA: Challenge Enterprises of Ghana, PO Box 5723, Accra.
Tel: (021) 222437/223249 Fax: (021) 226227 Email: ceg@africaonline.com.gh

HONG KONG: Cross Communications Ltd, 1/F, 562A Nathan Road, Kowloon.
Tel: 2780 1188 Fax: 2770 6229 Email: cross@crosshk.com

INDIA: Crystal Communications, 10-3-18/4/1, East Marredpalli, Secunderabad – 500026, Andhra Pradesh.
Tel/Fax: (040) 27737145 Email: crystal_edwj@rediffmail.com

KENYA: Keswick Books and Gifts Ltd, PO Box 10242-00400, Nairobi.
Tel: (254) 20 312639/3870125 Email: keswick@swiftkenya.com

MALAYSIA: Salvation Book Centre (M) Sdn Bhd, 23 Jalan SS 2/64, 47300 Petaling Jaya, Selangor.
Tel: (03) 78766411/78766797 Fax: (03) 78757066/78756360 Email: info@salvationbookcentre.com

Canaanland, No. 25 Jalan PJU 1A/41B, NZX Commercial Centre, Ara Jaya, 47301 Petaling Jaya, Selangor.
Tel: (03) 7885 0540/1/2 Fax: (03) 7885 0545 Email: info@canaanland.com.my

NEW ZEALAND: KI Entertainment, Unit 21 317-321 Woodpark Road, Smithfield,
New South Wales 2164, Australia.
Tel: 0 800 850 777 Fax: +612 9604 3699 Email: sales@kientertainment.com.au

NIGERIA: FBFM, Helen Baugh House, 96 St Finbarr's College Road, Akoka, Lagos.
Tel: (01) 7747429/4700218/825775/827264 Email: fbfm@hyperia.com

PHILIPPINES: OMF Literature Inc, 776 Boni Avenue, Mandaluyong City.
Tel: (02) 531 2183 Fax: (02) 531 1960 Email: gloadlaon@omflit.com

SINGAPORE: Alby Commercial Enterprises Pte Ltd, 95 Kallang Avenue #04-00,
AIS Industrial Building, 339420.
Tel: (65) 629 27238 Fax: (65) 629 27235 Email: marketing@alby.com.sg

SOUTH AFRICA: Struik Christian Books, 80 MacKenzie Street, PO Box 1144, Cape Town 8000.
Tel: (021) 462 4360 Fax: (021) 461 3612 Email: info@struikchristianmedia.co.za

SRI LANKA: Christombu Publications (Pvt) Ltd, Bartleet House, 65 Braybrooke Place, Colombo 2.
Tel: (9411) 2421073/2447665 Email: dhanad@bartleet.com

USA: David C Cook Distribution Canada, PO Box 98, 55 Woodslee Avenue, Paris, Ontario N3L 3E5, Canada.
Tel: 1800 263 2664 Email: swansons@cook.ca

CWR is a Registered Charity - Number 294387
CWR is a Limited Company registered in England - Registration Number 1990308

Day and Residential Courses
Counselling Training
Leadership Development
Biblical Study Courses
Regional Seminars
Ministry to Women
Daily Devotionals
Books and DVDs
Conference Centre

Trusted all Over the World

CWR HAS GAINED A WORLDWIDE reputation as a centre of excellence for Bible-based training and resources. From our headquarters at Waverley Abbey House, Farnham, England, we have been serving God's people for over 40 years with a vision to help apply God's Word to everyday life and relationships. The daily devotional *Every Day with Jesus* is read by nearly a million readers an issue in more than 150 countries, and our unique courses in biblical studies and pastoral care are respected all over the world. Waverley Abbey House provides a conference centre in a tranquil setting.

For free brochures on our seminars and courses, conference facilities, or a catalogue of CWR resources, please contact us at the following address:
CWR, Waverley Abbey House, Waverley Lane, Farnham, Surrey GU9 8EP, UK

Telephone: +44 (0)1252 784700
Email: mail@cwr.org.uk
Website: www.cwr.org.uk

CWR — Applying God's Word *to everyday life and relationships*

Dramatic new resource

Isaiah 40–66: Prophet of restoration
by John Houghton

God is a God of new beginnings, a God of second chances who takes no pleasure in punishment. However, profound lessons must be learned if the same errors are to be avoided in the future. Understand Isaiah's powerful message for each of us, that God is a holy God who cannot ignore sin, but One who also displays amazing grace and mercy, and who longs to enjoy restored relationship with us. These seven inspiring and challenging studies are perfect for individual or small-group use.
ISBN: 978-1-85345-550-6

Also available in the bestselling
Cover to Cover Bible Study Series

1 Corinthians
Growing a Spirit-filled church
ISBN: 978-1-85345-374-8

2 Corinthians
Restoring harmony
ISBN: 978-1-85345-551-3

1 Timothy
Healthy churches – effective Christians
ISBN: 978-1-85345-291-8

23rd Psalm
The Lord is my shepherd
ISBN: 978-1-85345-449-3

2 Timothy and Titus
Vital Christianity
ISBN: 978-1-85345-338-0

Ecclesiastes
Hard questions and spiritual answers
ISBN: 978-1-85345-371-7

Ephesians
Claiming your inheritance
ISBN: 978-1-85345-229-1

Esther
For such a time as this
ISBN: 978-1-85345-511-7

Fruit of the Spirit
Growing more like Jesus
ISBN: 978-1-85345-375-5

Genesis 1–11
Foundations of reality
ISBN: 978-1-85345-404-2

God's Rescue Plan
Finding God's fingerprints on human history
ISBN: 978-1-85345-294-9

Great Prayers of the Bible
Applying them to our lives today
ISBN: 978-1-85345-253-6

Hebrews
Jesus – simply the best
ISBN: 978-1-85345-337-3

Hosea
The love that never fails
ISBN: 978-1-85345-290-1

Isaiah 1–39
Prophet to the nations
ISBN: 978-1-85345-510-0

Isaiah 40–66
Prophet of restoration
ISBN: 978-1-85345-550-6

James
Faith in action
ISBN: 978-1-85345-293-2

Jeremiah
The passionate prophet
ISBN: 978-1-85345-372-4

£3.99 each (plus p&p)
Price correct at time of printing

Cover to Cover Every Day
Gain deeper knowledge of the Bible

Each issue of these bimonthly daily Bible-reading notes gives you insightful commentary on a book of the Old and New Testaments with reflections on a Psalm each weekend by Philip Greenslade.

Enjoy contributions from two well-known authors every two months, and over a five-year period you will be taken through the entire Bible.

ISSN: 1744-0114
Only £2.49 each (plus p&p)
£13.80 for annual UK subscription (6 issues)
£13.80 for annual email subscription
(available from www.cwr.org.uk/store)